CW00504490

FRENCH

Order with confidence from
French menus

French - English
Menulator

Throughout this book you will find several
"Tips and Helpful Phrases"

You may find it useful to read these before using
the dictionary section

For Special diets please see
Tips and Helpful Phrases on page 72

Introduction

When entering a restaurant in France you will generally wait to be seated. Greet the waiter with "Bonjour" followed by "pour deux (2) personnes s'il vous plait".

Manners are important in France, s'il vous plait Please Merci or merci beaucoup Thank you

They may ask for your drinks order "des boissons ?", "un aperitif ?" or "pour boire?"

Possible answers: -
De l'eau Water
Non Gazeuse Still
Gazeuse Sparkling
Un kir Chilled white wine with a flavoured syrup
Thé Tea
Café Coffee
Au lait With milk
Un verre de Vin Rouge Red wine
Un verre de Vin Blanc White wine
Une bouteille A bottle
Une carafe A carafe
Une Bière A beer
Un gin tonic Gin & tonic
Un Panaché Shandy
Une limonade A lemonade

Meals

Petit Déjeuner Breakfast
Déjeuner Lunch
Dîner Dinner

You should have "le menu/la carte" by now.
(Incidentally, menus are generally displayed outside the restaurant with prices).

**The menu may be presented as follows
(à la carte): -**

Les Entrées Starters
Hors d'oeuvre Starters
Les Poissons Fish course
Plat Principal/Plat Main course
Les Viandes Meat course

Accompaniments for your main meal may be listed separately as "accompagnements"

Les Fromages Cheeses
Les Desserts Desserts

You may find the following phrase on some menus:-

"Tous les desserts sont à commander en début de repas"
This means you have to order the sweet at the beginning of the meal

Forfaits
Fixed price menu

Set Value Menus/fixed price menus/plat du jour
Plate of the day

e.g. :-
Le menu a 27 Euro
Une entrée + un plat 20 Euro
Un plat + un dessert 18 Euro

These menus are a great way of simplifying the whole ordering process.

The waiter will ask you
Vous avez choisi? Have you chosen?

You then have to indicate to the waiter whether you are choosing a fixed price menu
e.g. le menu à 27 Euro **or À la carte**

After the meal:-
L'addition s'il vous plait The bill please
Service compris Service charge included, but small coins given in change are usually left in any event.
Je voudrais payer I would like to pay

On leaving the restaurant: -
Au revoir et Merci Goodbye and thank you

Abattis (Abats) Giblets (chicken livers etc.)
Ablette Type of fish
Abricot Apricot
Acarne Bream
Acavé Type of snail
Accompagnemen Trimmings, accompaniments
Accuniatu Meat stew (sheep/goat)
Aceline Type of Fish
Acerbe Sour
Achigan Bass
Acidulée Sharp/sour taste
Affinés Refined
Africaine Sauce with onions, and peppers
Agneau Lamb
Agrumes Citrus
Aigre Sour
Aigre-doux Sweet and sour
Aiglefin (fumé) Haddock (smoked)
Aïgo Bouido Provençal garlic soup with bread
Ail Garlic
Aioli Garlic sauce
Aiguillat Dogfish
Aiguillettes Thin slice (meat)
Aile Wing
Airelles Blueberries
Airelles rouges Cranberries
Albigeoise Potato and tomato accompaniment
Albran Wild duck
Albufera With truffles and stuffing
Alénois Cress
Algérienne With tomatoes and rice

Algues Seaweed
Algues Nories Type of seaweed
Aligot de Lozère Potato, cheese and garlic puree
Allemande sauce Egg and cream sauce
Allumettes Matchstick pastries
Alose Shad (selection of fish)
Alouette sans tète Beef Olive
Alouette Lark
Aloyau Sirloin
Alsacienne Frankfurters and sauerkraut
Amande Almond
Amandine Almond Tart
Amer Bitter
Américaine Lobster Cream Sauce
Amourettes Marrowbones
Amuse bouche Appetiser
Amuse-gueulé Hors-d'œuvre
Ananas Pineapple
Anoblie Noble/exclusive
Anchois Anchovy
Anchois de Norvège Sprat
Ancienne Old style (traditional)
Andalouse With sausage and peppers
Andouille Sausage (pork /chitterlings)
Andouillette Sausage (usually pork meat & seasoning)
Aneth Dill
Ange de mer Angel Fish
Angélique Angelica (green sugar decoration)
Angelo Monk fish
Anglaise (Crème or sauce) See Crème Anglaise
Anglaise, a l' Plain boiled
Anguille (fumé) Eel (smoked)

Anis Aniseed
Anone Custard apple
Antiboise Style of Antibes
Apogen Red mullet
Appellation Belonging to official production area (cheese/wine)
Appareil Type of stuffing
Arachide Peanut
Arborio (Risotto) Type of risotto
Archiduc Cream, mushroom & cognac sauce
Arc-en-ciel (truite) Rainbow (trout)
Arêtes (de poisson) (fish) Bones
Argenteuil Served with asparagus
Ariégeoise With pickled pork and cabbage
Alésienne With aubergine and tomatoes
Armoricaine With Brandy, onions, white wine sauce
Aromatisé Flavoured/spiced
Arrosé Celebration
Arrow-root Arrowroot
Artichaut Artichoke
Asperge Asparagus
Aspic Aspic
Assaisonné Seasoned
Assaisonnement Seasoning
Assiette Plate (e.g. assiette des fromages = plate of cheeses)
Assiette de viandes grillées Mixed grill
Assortie Assorted
Atoca Cranberry
Aubergine Aubergine (eggplant)
Aubourg Type of fish
Aujourd'hui Today
Aumônier Pouch shaped filled pancake
Auriol Mackerel
Aurore Tomato puree

Autour Around
Autruche Ostrich
Avec With
Aveline Filbert (Nut)
Avocat Avocado
Avoine Oats
Aythya Wild duck

Tips & Helpful Phrases

Towns and areas lend their names to dishes

e.g.
au Chinon, Provençal, Bordelaise, Guérande, Niçoise, Nantaise etc. which generally denote a style of dish or the area in which the dish has derived.

aise/oise/ine these endings can mean in the style of, flavoured by or accompanied with. Plurals and genders often give the words different endings.

Chou (x) Cabbage (s)
Délicieux Delicious, referring to a masculine item.
Délicieuse Delicious, referring to a feminine item.

Badiane Aniseed flavoured spirit
Badoise With bacon, red cabbage, cherries and potatoes
Baguette French Bread
Baie de sureau Elderberry
Baises Reduced down
Bajoues Pig cheeks
Bakeofe Hotpot
Ballottine Faggot
Balsamique Balsamic
Bamboche Bamboo shoot
Banane Banana
Banquière With mushroom and dumplings
Bar Sea bass
Barbarin Type of fish
Barbejuans Pastry parcels of spinach & herbs
Barbet Barbet
Barboteur Duck
Barbouche Tripe with couscous
Barbue Brill (fish)
Bardane Burdock
Barde Bacon slice
Barigoule Type of mushroom
Barquette Boat shaped pastry
Basilic Basil
Basses Calories Low Calories
Basquaise, à la Basque style, ham, peppers and tomatoes
Bat Fish tail
Bâtarde sauce Egg, butter and lemon
Bateau Boat
Batelière With crayfish and mushrooms
Bâtonnets Batons (vegetables)
Battu Beaten
Baudroie Monk Fish

Baux de Provence Type of mushroom
Bavaroise Bavarian
Bavaroise sauce With crayfish and cream
Bavette Flank
Béarnaise White sauce
Béatilles Sweetbreads
Beauharnais Potato and artichoke
Bécasse Woodcock
Bécasse de mer Red mullet
Béchamel White sauce
Bêche-de-mer Sea cucumber
Beignets Fritter
Beignet de banane Banana fritter
Beignet viennois Plain doughnut
Belle Hélène Cold Chocolate sauce
Bercy sauce Fish sauce with butter & parsley
Bergamote Bergamot
Bernacle Limpet
Berny With lentils and truffles
Bête rousse Young boar
Bête de compagnie Young wild boar
Bétail Cattle
Bette Chard
Betterave Beetroot
Beurre Butter
Beurre noir Butter (dark seasoned)
Beurre noire Browned butter, vinegar and lemon juice
Beurre noisette Brown butter
Biche Doe (venison)
Bichiques Type of fish
Bifteck Beef steak
Bigarade (sauce) Sauce made with remains of duck and fruit
Bigorneau Winkle

Billy by Mussel soup
Biologique Organic
Biscotte Crispbread
Biscuits Biscuits
Biscuits a la cuillère Sponge fingers
Biset Pigeon
Bisque (de Homard) Thin soup (lobster)
Bitok Beef rissole
Bizontine With cauliflower and potato
Blanc White
Blanchaille Whitebait
Blanchi Whitened
Blanquette Cream sauce
Blavet Type of mushroom
Blé Wheat
Blennie cagnette Fish
Blette (vert de) Chard
Bleuets Cornflowers
Bleus Blue cheese
Blinis Small thick pancake
Bloc Slab
Blondie Whiten
Bœuf Beef
Bœuf de conserve Corned Beef
Bogue Type of fish
Bohémienne With rice and tomatoes
Bois Wood (forest)
Boitelle Minced mushrooms
Bol Bowl
Bolets Type of mushroom
Bombe Ice cream
Bonbonnière Type of serving dish
Bonbons Sweets
Bon-Henri Wild spinach

B

Bon - Bou

Bonne femme Cooked with potatoes and leeks
Bonite Type of tuna
Bordelaise Sauce with red wine, mushrooms, shallots
Bordure Ring shaped dish
Bortsh Russian beetroot soup
Boucan Smoked meat
Bouche Mouth
Boucher Butcher
Bouchée à la reine Vol-au-vent with mushrooms and cream
Bouchon Cap
Bougras Vegetable soup
Boulangerie Bakery
Boule de glace Scoop of ice cream
Bouillabaisse Fish Stew
Bouilleture Eel stew
Bouilli Boiled
Bouillinade Fish and potato pie
Bouillon Broth
Boudins Type of sausage/pudding
Baudroie Angler fish
Bouillon Stock/broth
Boule Crusty loaf
Boulette de pâte Dumpling
Boulette de viande Meatball
Bouquet rose Prawns
Bourdelot With bacon and carrots
Bourigoule Type of mushroom
Bourgeois Family style
Bourguignonne Red wine, mushroom, onion sauce
Bourrache Borage (herb)
Bourride Fish with Garlic mayonnaise sauce

14

Bourse a Berger Lambs lettuce
Braisé Braised
Brancas sauce Sauce with veal
Branche Stalk
Brandade Cod in cream
Brande Puree
Brasillé Grilled
Brebis Ewe
Brejauda soupe Soup with cabbage and bacon
Brème Bream
Brési Type of beef jerky
Bresse Region in France famous for chicken
Breton With leeks and mushrooms
Bretonneau Turbot
Bretzel Pretzel
Brik Pasty with egg and tuna
Brioche Cold toast
Broccana Sausage and veal pate
Broche Skewer (spit roast)
Brochet Pike
Brocheton Young pike
Brochette Skewer/kebab
Brocolis Broccoli
Brouillé Scrambled
Brouillade Mixture
Broutard Young goat
Brugnon Nectarine
Brûlé Burnt
Brune Brown
Brunoise Soup with shredded vegetables
Bruxelloise With brussels and chicory
Bucard Cockle

Buccin Whelk
Bûche de Noel Christmas log
Bûcheron Forester Style
Bugne Fritter
Buisson Tree/bush like display

Tips & Helpful Phrases

Du jour Of the day (today)
De pays Local
De la maison Of the house

Pour commencer To start
Pour suivre To follow
Pour finir To finish

USEFUL NOTES:

Cabécou Goats cheese, usually warm
Cabillaud Cod
Cabiros Young goat
Cabot Chub
Cabri Kid goat
Cacahuète Peanut
Cacao Cocoa
Café Coffee
Café Liégeoise Iced coffee with cream
Cagouilles Snails
Caïeu Large mussel
Cailettes Faggots
Caille Quail
Cailletot Turbot
Caillette Pigs liver sausage
Caisse (en) Wrapped with pastry
Cake Fruitcake
Calamars Squid
Calappe Crustacean
Camard Gurnard
Cambridge sauce Spicy sauce with anchovies
Camérani With truffles and liver
Campagnarde Country style
Campagne Country
Canard Duck
Canard siffleur Widgeon
Canaron Gurnard
Cancaiaise With shrimps and oysters
Cancale Type of oyster
Caneton Rouennaise Duck cooked with wine and brandy
Cangalaise With shrimps and oysters
Canneberge Cranberry
Cannelle Cinnamon
Caneton Duckling

Canette Duckling
Canon Tube/rolled
Cantaloup Cantaloupe Melon
Capitaine Carp
Caprice Cake
Capucin Hare
Caqhuse Braised pork
Caquelon Small pot dish
Caramel Caramel
Carbonnade Beef stew with beer
Cardeau Sardine
Cardinal Shellfish with truffles
Cardinal sauce Fish sauce with lobster flavoured butter
Cardine Type of fish
Carottes Carrots
Carrelet Plaice
Cantine Dish (or dining room)
Caprés Capers
Carbonade (de bœuf) Braised with onions and beer
Cardamome Cardamom
Cari Curry
Caroube Type of bean
Carpaccio Wafer thin slices of raw beef or tuna
Carpe Carp
Carpion Trout
Carré Rack
Carrelet Plaice
Carrots Vichy Carrots in butter and parsley
Carvi Caraway
Casher Kosher
Cassé Broken

Cassis Blackcurrant
Cassoulette Casserole
Cassoulette flamande Casserole of beans, pork, sausage and goose
Castiglione With ham, risotto & mushrooms
Catalane With tomatoes, olives & garlic
Catigau d'anguilles Eel stew
Cavaillon Honeydew Melon
Caviar Caviar
Caviar d'aubergine Pureed aubergines
Cavour With chicken livers
Cayuga Duck
Cebéttes Salad Onions
Cédrat Citron
Céleri Celery
Céleri-rave Celeriac
Cendre Embers
Cèpe Type of mushroom (porcini)
Cèpe glaces Meringue, ice cream and warm chocolate
Céréales Cereals
Cerf Venison
Cerfeuil Chervil (herb)
Cerise Cherry
Cerise noire Black cherry
Cervelle Brains
Cervelas Saveloy
Cevenole With bacon and chestnuts
Chaboisseau Type of fish
Chabot Chub
Chair à sausisse Sausage meat
Chalonnaise Kidney Tarts
Chambord sauce Fish and red wine sauce
Champignon Mushroom
Champignon de Paris Button mushrooms

Champignon farcis Stuffed mushrooms
Chanoinesse Carrots, truffles and cream
Chanterelle Type of mushroom
Chantilly Cream (whipped)
Chaource Type of cheese
Chapeau Pie crust
Chapelure Breadcrumbs
Chapon Capon (chicken)
Chapon de mer Scorpion fish
Charbon de bois Charcoal
Charbonnier Type of fish
Charcuterie Delicatessen
Charlotte Moulded sponge cake
Chariot Trolley
Charolais Breed of cow
Charollaise Turnip and cauliflower puree
Chartres With lettuce and mushrooms
Chartreuse Mixture of vegetables/meats
Chartreuse de légumes Layered
vegetables with stuffing
Chasseur Red wine, garlic, mushroom
and tomato sauce
Châtaigne Sweet Chestnut
Chateaubriand (t) Fillet of beef
Châtelaine With artichokes and chestnuts
Chaud Hot
Chaudée Apple tart
Chaud-froid Jelly/aspic
Chaud-froid blanche Cold veloute sauce
Chaud-froid brûne Jellied sauce and
Madeira wine
Chaud-froid poisson Jellied fish dish
Chaud-froid volaille Jellied poultry dish
Chaudrée Chowder (thick soup)
Chausson Pastry turnover
Chavanne Chub
Chemise Coating/skin (shirt)

Chemitré Type of waffle
Chêne Oak
Cheval Horse
Chevaux d'ange Angel hair (pasta)
Chevesne Chub
Chèvre Goat
Chevreuil Venison (deer)
Chevreuse With artichokes and truffles
Chevrier Green haricot bean
Chich Kebab
Chiche Chick pea
Chicon Chicory
Chicorée Endive
Chien de mer Dogfish
Chiffonnade Garnish folds or strips
Chinchard Horse mackerel
Chine China
Chinoise Chinese
Chipirone Squid
Chipirons à l'encre Stewed squid in ink
Chips Potato crisps
Chivry sauce With onions and white wine
Chocolat Chocolate
Choesels Belgian stew with tripe
Choix Choice
Choron With artichoke and peas
Choron sauce Egg and wine sauce
Chou (x) Cabbage (s)
Choucroute Pickled cabbage/sauerkraut
Choucroute garné Sauerkraut with sausages
Chou a la crème Cream puff/éclair
Chou-fleur Cauliflower
Chou-navet Swede
Chou-rave Kohlrabi
Chou de Bruxelles Brussel sprouts
Chou de chine Chinese leaves
Chou de mer Sea kale
Chou de Milan Savoy cabbage
Chouée Boiled green cabbage
Chou marin Sea kale
Chou pomme White cabbage

Choux au fromage Cheese puffs
Ciboule Spring onions
Ciboulette Chives
Cidre Cider
Cigarettes Russes Hazelnut cream filled wafer tube
Cimier Rump
Cinabre Cinnabar
Citronelle Lemon grass
Citron Lemon
Citron vert Lime
Citrouille Pumpkin
Cive Spring onion
Civelle Young eel
Civet Stew (game)
Civet de langouste Lobster stew
Civet de lièvre Jugged hare
Civette Chives
Clafoutis Baked in batter with fruit
Clairette Lambs lettuce
Clamart With peas and artichoke hearts
Clermont With onions and chestnuts
Clou de girofle Clove
Clovisse Clam
Cochon Pig
Cochon de lait Suckling pig
Cocktail de crevettes Prawn cocktail
Cocotte Casserole
Coeur Heart
Coeur a la crème Heart shaped curd cheese desert
Coeur d'artichauts Artichoke hearts
Coeur d'Arras Thin chocolate biscuits
Coeur de filet Middle of fillet
Coing Quince (fruit)
Colbert Fish in breadcrumbs
Colin Hake
Collet de mouton Neck of mutton
Collioure sauce Mayonnaise with anchovies
Collop Escalope
Colombe Dove

Colvert Mallard (duck)
Commande (sur) Request (on)
Commodore Mussels, crayfish and dumplings
Compotée Stewed (fruit)
Compris Included
Concassée Crushed/chopped
Concombre Cucumber
Concorde With potatoes, carrots and peas
Condé With rice
Confit Preserve
Confit d'oie Preserved goose
Confiture Puree
Confiture Jam
Confiture d'oranges Marmalade
Congelés Frozen food
Congre Conger eel
Coing Quince
Conserves Preserves
Consommé Clear soup
Consommé Jellied (fruit)
Consommé à l'œuf Clear soup with raw egg
Conti With lentils and bacon
Contrefilet Steak
Conty With lentils
Copeau Grated
Coppa Type of sausage
Coprin Type of mushroom
Coq au vin Chicken in red wine
Coq d'inde Turkey
Coq de bruyère Wood grouse
Coq Faisan Cock pheasant
Coq rayée Clam
Coques Cockles
Coquillages Shellfish
Coquilles St Jacques Scallops in a half shell with creamy sauce
Coquelicot Poppy
Corbeau Rook
Coriandre Coriander
Cornichon Gherkin

Côte Coast line (area)
Côte (d'agneau) Chop (Lamb)
Côtes Ribs
Côtes de la Manche Around the English channel
Côtier Coastal
Cotisé Served Together
Côtelettes Cutlets
Cotriade Fish Stew with onions and potato
Cou neck
Coucoumelle Type of mushroom
Courcouzelle Courgette
Couenne Pork rind
Coulemelle Type of mushroom
Coulibiac Fish pie stuffed with rice and egg
Coulibiac de poulet Chicken pie
Coulis Sauce
Coup Dish (bowl)
Coupe Cup (for fruit)
Couper To cut
Copeaux Chunks
Corail Red coloured
Corolle Petals
Coup Jacques Fruit liqueur and ice cream
Courge Squash/marrow
Court Short (reduced)
Court bouillon Fish stock
Cousinât Chestnut soup
Cousinette Spinach soup
Couteau Razor fish
Covenne Crackling
Crabe Crab
Crameou Shell-less crab
Crapaudine De-boned (fowl)
Craquant Crusty
Craquelot de Dunkirk Smoked herring
Craquelin Cream cracker
Craquelin Type of apple pie/biscuit
Crécy With carrots

Crème Cream (or a white coffee)
Crème Anglais Custard
Crème bordelaise Prune and cream puree
Crème Brûlée Set custard with burnt brown sugar coating
Crème caprice Meringue and cream
Crème caramel Caramel custard
Crème chantilly Whipped cream
Crème douce Sweet cream
Crème d'asperges Cream of asparagus soup
Crème de tomates Cream of tomato soup
Crème de volaille Cream of chicken soup
Crème fraîche Soured cream
Crème renversée Set custard
Crémeux Creamy
Crèment Creamed
Crème vichyssoise Potato and leek pancake
Créole With rice, pepper and tomatoes
Crêpe Pancake
Crêpe dentelles Cigar-shaped pancakes
Crépinette Small sausage with seasoning
Crêpe Suzette Pancake with orange sauce
Cresson Cress
Cresson de fontaine Watercress
Cressonnière Made with watercress
Creuse Oyster
Crevettes (grise) Shrimp
Crevettes (rose) Prawn
Criée Market fresh
Croissant Flaky sweet breakfast bun
Cromesquis Fried meat balls
Croquant Crunchy
Croque-madame Cheese and Ham toastie with fried egg
Croque-monsieur Cheese and Ham toastie
Coussin Cushion
Croustade Bread /pastry case
Croustillant Crisp
Croûte (en croûte) In a pastry case
Croûte de sel Crust of salt

Crottin de chèvre Small round goats cheese
Cru Raw
Crudités Raw sliced vegetables as a hors d'oeuvre
Crumble Crumble
Crustacés Shellfish
Cuillère Spoon
Cuisse Thigh/Leg
Cuisses de grenouilles Frogs Legs
Cuisait Cooked
Cuisine Cookery
Cuissot Haunch
Cuit (e) Cooked
Cuit à la vapeur Steamed
Cul blanc Snipe
Cul de veau Veal haunch
Cullis Shrimp soup
Culotte de boeuf Beef rump
Cumin Cumin (spicy seed)
Cumin des prés Caraway
Curaçao Seville orange liqueur
Curcuma Turmeric
Cussy With mushrooms and kidneys

Tips & Helpful Phrases

Froide (s) Cold
Chaud (e) Hot
Tiède Warm

Printemps Spring
Été Summer
Automne Autumn
Hiver Winter

Dacquoise Fruit and cream meringue
Damier Chequerboard(assorted)
Dame blanche Ice cream with peaches and pineapple
Dame blanch fruits Poached peaches on ice cream
Dard Freshwater fish
Darne Steak of fish
Darne d'anguilles Eel Steak
Darne de saumon Salmon steak
Datte Date
Datte fourrée Stuffed date
Daube Casserole with red wine
Daubière Casserole
Daumont With crayfish
Dauphine (ois) Cream garlic sauce style
Daurade Bream
Découpe Carved
Découverte Unveiled
Dégustation Tasty
Délice Delight/speciality
Délicieux (se) Delicious
Demi Half
Demi-deuil With white sauce
Demoiselle Eel like fish
Demoiselle (tarte de) Fruit tart
Dentelle Lace
Derval With artichokes
Descar With chicken and potato
Dés Diced
Desséché Dried
Désossé Filleted
Diable Hot sauce
Diablotin White sauce with bread and cheese
Diane sauce Vegetable and cream sauce
Dieppoise With mussels and shrimps
Dijonnaise With mustard
Dijonnaise sorbet Water-ice with cassis liqueur

Dinde Turkey
Diplomate pouding Sponge with custard and fruit
Dodine Boned and stuffed
Dolmades Stuffed vine leaves
Donax Small fish
Donzelle Small eel
Dorade Bream
Dorée John Dory (Fish)
Dorer To brown
Doria With truffles and asparagus
Dormeur Crab
Dos Backs
Double Chub
Douce Soft
Doucette Lambs lettuce
Douillon Fruit dumpling
Douillons normande Apple/pear turnover
Doux Soft
Douzaine Dozen
Dragées Sugared Almonds
Dressée Dressed with
Duabarry With cauliflower
Dubley With potatoes and mushrooms
Duchesse Piped mashed potato
Duglère With wine, tomatoes and cream
Duo Two of
Dur (e) Hard boiled
Duroe With new potatoes
Duse With potato, tomotoes and french beans
Duxelles White wine sauce/mushroom stuffing

Eau Water
Ecaille Peel
Ecarlate Salted pork/beef
Échalotes Shallot/onions
Echassier Type of water fowl
Echine Backbone
Éclade Mussels with pine needles
Écorces Peel (fruit)
Écorce de citron Lemon peel
Écossaise sauce Cream sauce with French beans and vegetables
Ecumé Foam/froth
Ecrasées Crushed
Ecrevisses Cray fish
Écrevisse à la nege Crayfish in wine and vegetable sauce
Effeuillé Strips
Effiloche Shredded
Églefin Haddock
Elbot Type of fish
Emiettée Crumbled
Emincée Sliced thin
Émulsionné Emulsion (sauce)
Emulsionne a l'huile Olive oil and water mix
Encornet Squid
Encre de seiche Cuttle fish ink
Endive Chicory
Endive au jambon Chicory with ham baked in oven
Enrobé Coated
Entrecôte Beef Steak
Entrecôte minute Thin steak
Entrecuisse Thigh of poultry/game
Entrelardé Streaky bacon
Entremet Side dish
Entrements Cream dessert
Entremont Salé Savoury
Environ There abouts
Epaule Shoulder

Éperian Smelt
Épi de mais Corn on the cob
Epices Spices
Épigramme Lamb stew
Épigramme d'agneau Lamb and egg bread crumbed
Épinard Spinach
Épinevinette Spice
Épinoche Small river fish
Epis de mais Sweet corn
Éplucher To peel
Equile Sand eel
Erable (jus d') Maple syrup
Escabèche With onions, chilli, herbs and peppers
Escalopes Flattened slice of meat
Escalope de veau Veal escalope
Escalopines Nugget of meat
Escargot Snails
Escargot de mer Winkle
Espagne Spain
Espadon Sword Fish
Espagnole With tomatoes and onions
Estouffade Braised dish
Estouffat Pork and bean casserole
Etouffée Steamed/braised
Estuaire Estuary
Estragon Tarragon
Esturgeon Sturgeon
Étoile Star
Étrille Crab
Etuvée Braised
Eventail Shaped like fan
Excelsior With potatoes and lettuce

Façon Style
Faínes Beech nuts
Faisan Pheasant
Faisselle Curd cheese
Fanes de navets Turnip tops
Fanfre Pilot fish
Far Flan with raisins/prunes
Far breton Shortbread of prune
Farci (es) Stuffed
Farcon Sweet pudding of potatoes
Farée Stuffed cabbage
Farfelles Pasta
Farine Flour
Far poitevin Herb and vegetable stuffing inside cabbage leaves
Farz Dumpling
Faséole Haricot bean
Faubonne ~Bean and vegetable soup
Fauves Wild
Faux Filet Sirloin steak
Faverolle Haricot bean
Favorite With asparagus and truffles
Favorite purée French bean puree
Fécule de mais Cornflour
Fenouil Fennel
Féra Lake Salmon
Fermier Free range (of the farm)
Fermière With vegetables
Feu Fire
Feuillantine Puff Pastry
Feuille Leaf
Feuille de laurier Bay leaf
Feuilleté Pastry
Fève Broad Bean
Fiadone Lemon cheese cake
Ficelle Bread (very long thin loaf)
Ficelle picarde Pancake filled with ham with white sauce
Figues Figs
Filet Fillet

Finement Finely
Fines herbes Mixed herbs
Flageolets Flageolet Beans
Flambé Flamed
Flaiche Pastry tart
Flan Baked custard
Fleur Flower
Flet Flounder (flat fish)
Flétan Halibut
Floc Blob
Flocons Flakes
Florentine With spinach
Florilège specially selected
Foie Liver
Foie gras Liver paté
Fondant au chocolat Chocolate fudge
Fondantes Tender
Fondue Fondue
Forêt- noir Black forest (gateau)
Forestière Accompanied by bacon,
mushrooms and fried potatoes
Fougasse Flat bread
Four Oven
Fourrée Filled
Frais, fraîche Fresh
Fraise Strawberry
Fraîcheur Cold/Fresh
Framboise Raspberries
Frangipane Pastry almond and cream
filling
Friand Puff pastry filled with meat
Fricandeau Braised veal
Fricassé Stew
Frisée Endive salad
Fritots Deep fried items
Frit (ure) Fried
Frites Chips (English)
Friture de poisons Mixed fried fish
Frivole Frivolity

Fruits de mer Seafood
Fruit secs Dried fruit
Froid Cold
Fromage Cheese
Fromage Blanc Cows milk cheese low fat
Fromage de tête Brawn
Fromage frais Soft cheese
Froment Wheat
Fruits Fruits
Feuillantine Puff Pastry
Feuille Leaf
Fumé Smoked

Tips & Helpful Phrases

If you want to ask for something such as butter, milk or water you can not just say beurre, lait or eau,

you must ask for some butter, milk or water, du beurre or du lait or de l'eau.

USEFUL NOTES:

33

Tips & Helpful Phrases

Salade not always
lettuce and tomatoes

Sur commande (made) to order

Selon arrivage if available

USEFUL NOTES:

Galette Pancake
Gambas Large prawns
Garamasala Chutney
Garbure Vegetable and ham Soup
Garne With vegetables
Garniture Garnish/salad or vegetables
Gaspacho Cold Soup (Spanish)
Gâteau Cake
Gâteau au fromage blanc Cheese cake
Gâteau mousseline Sponge cake
Gâteau de Noël Christmas cake
Gaufre Waffle
Gaufrette Wafer
Géante Giant
Gelée Jelly
Genièvre Juniper Berry
Génois Type of sponge cake
Germe de Blé Wheat germ
Germe de luzerne Alfalfa Sprouts
Germe de soja Bean sprouts
Gésiers Gizzards
Gibier Game
Gigot Leg e.g. Lamb/mutton (sometimes a portion of fish)
Gingembre Ginger
Girolles Type of mushroom
Gîte à la noix Silverside
Glace Ice cream
Glacé Iced
Glaçage Icing
Glaçon Ice cube
Gnocchi Parmentier Potato Dumplings
Gombo Small type of gherkin
Gougère Pastry ring with cheese
Goujon Gudgeon (Type of fish)
Goujon Strips (chicken, fish etc)
Goujonette Small strips
Gourmande Large portion
Goulue Greedy
Gousse Pod or bean
Gousses Cloves/Pods

Goût Taste
Goûteux Tasty
Goyave Guava (fruit)
Grain Seed
Grains de genièvre Juniper Berries
Graisse Grease
Grand-mère Home made
Granité Sorbet
Granit Papillotes Chocolate in foil wrapping
Gras Fatty
Gras Double Tripe
Gratin Browned (as in under grill)
Gravlax (see saumon gravlax)
Grenade Pomegranate
Grenadin de veau Dish of larded/glazed
fillets of veal
Grenaille Small pieces
Grenouilles Frogs
Gribiche Egg and herb sauce
Grillade Grilling
Griottes Cherry like fru
Grive Thrush
Grondin Gurnard (fish)
Groseilles Red or white currants
Groseille a maquereau Gooseberry
Gros sel Rock salt
Grosse Fève Broad bean and pepper salad
Guimauve Marshmallow

Habillée Dressed/covered with
Habit Dressing
Hachée Minced (steak)
Hachis Minced/ground up
Hareng Herring
Harenguet Sprat
Haricots Beans
Haricots Vert Green Beans
Harissa Hot chilli puree
Haché (steak haché) Burger
Hélène fruits Fruit with chocolate and ice cream
Hélène, poire belle Pear with chocolate and ice cream
Hochepot Mutton and vegetable soup
Hollandaise Seasoned egg sauce
Homard Lobster (Hure de)
Hongroise Spicy fresh cream sauce
Houmous Mashed chick peas and garlic
Huile Oil
Huile de colza Rapeseed oil
Huile d'olive Olive Oil
Huîtres Oysters
Hypocras Type of liqueur (melon, pear)

Igname Yam
Iles Flottantes Soft meringue floating on custard
Impératrice With rice
Impériale With truffles, liver and kidneys
Incorpore Blended/Mixed
Indienne Indian Style (curry)
Infusion Brew
Iode White wine sauce
Iridée Edible seaweed
Ismail bayeedi With aubergines, rice and tomatoes
Ivoire With cream sauce and mushrooms

Tips & Helpful Phrases

Frit (e) Fried
À la poêle (poêle (e) Pan fried
Rôtie Roast
Fume Smoked
Au four Baked
Grillé (e) Grilled
Poché (e) Poached
À la Vapeur Steamed
À l'eau Boiled

USEFUL NOTES:

Jacques Apple pancakes
Jalousies Flaky pastry cakes
Jambon Ham
Jambon blanc (slice of) Boiled ham
Jambon de Bayonne Smoked Ham
Jambon de pays Local Ham
Jambon poché Boiled Ham
Jambon Serrano Spanish Ham
Jambonneau Pigs knuckle
Jambonnette Type of sausage/terrine
Japonaise Ice bombe pudding
Jardin Garden
Jardinière Served with vegetables
Jarret Knuckle/shank
Jaseur Waxwing, an edible bird
Jaune d'œuf Egg yolk
Jessica With artichokes, bone marrow,
mushrooms and shallots
Jésus Type of sausage
Jeune Young
Joinville With mushrooms, shrimps and
truffles
Joue (de porc) Cheek (of pig)
Jubilée, cerises Cherries flamed in brandy
Judic With tomatoes, lettuce and potatoes
Julienne Strips
Jus Juice
Jus corsé Corsican juice
Juste Just (only)
Jussiére With onions, lettuce and carrots

Tips & Helpful Phrases

Petit (e) Small
Grand (e) Large
a, au, aux
This can mean of, with, to or at
Son/Sa/Ses It's
Ou Or
Sur On
Sous Under
Climatisé Air conditioned

USEFUL NOTES:

Kaki Date plum
Kalerii Type of pork brawn (Alsace)
Kaltschale Fruit salad with liqueur
Kasher Kosher
Keftede Veal or pork and potato rissole
Kig ha farz Beef stew with dumplings
Kilkis Norwegian anchovies
Kirsch Cherry liqueur
Koulibiac Fish pie stuffed with rice and egg
Kromeskies Little meat balls
Kumquat Kumquat (very small orange)

Tips & Helpful Phrases

Meal Times

Petit déjeuner Breakfast
0700 - 0900
Déjeuner Lunch
1200 - 1400
Dîner Dinner
1900 - 2200

Many French families eat in restaurants for
Sunday Lunch - You should try to book in
advance if you wish to eat at this time.

And remember... Never hurry your meal

Tips & Helpful Phrases

Auriez - vous une table de libre
Could we have a table
L'exterieur Outside
Prés de la fenêtre By the window
Dans la section fumeurs In the
smoking area
Dans la section non-fumeurs
In the non-smoking area

USEFUL NOTES:

Lache Small delicate sea fish
Lagopède Grouse
Lait Milk
Laitances Soft roes
Lait entier Full cream milk
Laitance Roe
Laitue Lettuce
Lamballe With mushrooms, truffles, port and cream
Lamproie Eel - like fish
Lançon Sand-eel
Lande (s)(aise) Of the land/moors
Langoustine Large type of prawn
Langouste Type of crayfish
Langue Tongue
Languedocienne With mushrooms, aubergines and potatoes
Lapin Rabbit
Lapereau Young rabbit
Lard Bacon
Lard de poitrine Streaky Bacon
Lardons Cubed pieces (bacon)
Lavallière With truffles, lambs' sweetbreads and truffles
Lavande Lavender
Lavaret A salmon-like fish
Laurier Bay leaves
Leberwurst Liver sausage
Lèche Thin slice of meat or bread
Legumes Vegetables
Légumineuses Pulses (lentils, beans etc)
Léger (e) Light (not heavy)
Légèrement Lightly
Lentilles Lentils
Lentins Type of mushroom
Letchi Lychee
Liche Tuna-like fish
Lié Together with
Lieu Jeune Pollack

Lieu Noir Saithe/Coley (fish)
Lièvre Hare
Ligurienne With tomatoes, risotto and potatoes
Limande Dab (Small flat fish)
Limandelle Plaice-like fish
Limande-sole Lemon sole
Limousine With red cabbage
Lingue Ling (fish)
Lingots Ingots
Lisette Small Mackerel
Lit Bed
Litchi Lychee
Lobe Lob
Loche Loach, a freshwater fish
Longchamp Broth with sorrel, vermicelli and peas
Longe Loin (Pork etc)
Lonzo Herb flavoured pork
Lorette With chicken croquettes, asparagus and truffles
Lotte Monk Fish
Loubine Regional name for grey mullet
Loup Bass
Lou trebuc Preserved goose or pork
Lyonnaise With onions

Macaron Macaroon (biscuit)
Macaronade Beef stew with noodles
Macédoine Mixture of (chopped)
Mâche Lambs Lettuce
Macis Mace
Macreuse Strong flavoured wild duck
Madeleine Small flat sponge cake
Madère (sauce) Madeira and butter sauce
Madrilène With tomatoes
Magistère Type of soup
Maigre Thin, lean
Maillot With carrots, turnips, beans and lettuce
Maintenon With creamy white mushroom sauce
Maïs Corn
Maison House
Maître d'hôtel Butter with salt, pepper, lemon juice and parsley
Magret Breast (fowl)/ Best cut of fish or meat
Malard Mallard
Maltaise sauce Egg and butter sauce with orange juice
Manchons Pasty
Mange-touts Young peas with pods
Mangue Mango
Mante de mer Squill fish
Maquereau Mackerel
Maraîchère Salad/Vegetables
Marc Grape Brandy
Marcassin Young boar
Marchet Garden
Marchand de vin Red wine sauce
Maréchal With asparagus tips and truffles
Marengo With crayfish, eggs and brandy
Marennes Variety of oyster
Mariage Thick meat soup with fish garnish
Marigny With artichoke hearts, sweet corn and potatoes
Marinière White wine, onions marinade

Marbré Layers of
Marcassin Young Boar
Marché Market
Marée Fresh Sea Fish
Mariné Marinated
Marivaux With potatoes and mixed
vegetables
Marjolaine Marjoram
Marmite Cooking Pot (stew or soup)
Marocaine With rice, courgettes, sweet
peppers
Marouette Rail, a small bird
Marquise Frozen Desert (sweet)
Marron Sweet chestnut
Marron glacées Candied chestnuts
Marvel Fritter
Mascarpone Type of cheese used in
cheesecake
Mascotte With artichoke hearts, truffles
and potatoes
Masqué Covered with
Masséna With artichoke hearts and bone
marrow
Massepain Marzipan
Matafan Pancake
Matefaim Thick pancake
Matelot Fish Stew
Matignon With artichoke hearts and
lettuce
Mauviette Lark
Méchoui Spit roasted lamb
Méchouia Mixed vegetable salad
Mélange Blended./mixed
Mêlasse Treacle
Méli-mélo Medley
Mélongène Aubergine
Menthe Mint
Mentonnaise Courgette, artichoke, rice and
olives
Mer Sea

Merguez Spicy meat sausage
Merlan Whiting
Merle Blackbird
Merlu Hake
Merluche Dried hake
Mérou Grouper
Mesclun Salad leaves
Meuils Grey mullet
Meunière Floured and fried
Meurette Red wine fish stew
Mi-amer (slightly bitter)
Mi-cuit Parboiled
Miel Honey
Mignardise Dainty/small
Mignon Fillet
Mijoté Simmered
Mijoter Simmer
Mignardise Type of biscuit
Mikado Chocolate biscuit
Mikado With curried rice, soya shoots in sauce
Milanaise Pasta sauce with tomato and parmesan
Milla aux pommes Apple cake
Millefeuille Creamy puff pastry
Mimolette Type of cheese
Mirabeau Olives, anchovies and tarragon
Mirabelle Yellow plumb (small)
Mirepoi Diced vegetables
Miroir Mirror
Mise Something suitable
Mise en bouche Appetiser
Moderne With mixed vegetables
Moelle Bone marrow
Mogettes Red beans
Mogettes French beans with butter and cream
Moka Dark chocolate (Mocha)
Monie borgne Type of cod

Monte Mounted
Monteglas Truffles, foie gras & pickled tongue
Montgolfière White wine, truffles and mushrooms
Montpensier Asparagus tips and truffles
Monselet Artichoke hearts and truffles
Morbihan Variety of oyster
Morelle Aubergine
Morilles Type of mushroom
Morceaux Pieces
Mornay White cheese sauce
Mortadelle Large pork sausage
Morue Cod
Mostelle Mediterranean fish
Mouclade Creamy mussel stew
Moules Mussels
Moulu Ground
Mouillettes Bread fingers
Mouloucoutani Mulligatawny soup or dish, curry flavoured
Mousse (use) Mousse
Mousse (élime) Mousse
Mousseline Puree
Mousseline (sauce) Creamy hollandaise sauce
Moutarde Mustard
Mouton Mutton
Mulet Mullet
Mûr Ripe
Mures Blackberry/Mulberry
Mure de ronce Blackberry
Murène Moray eel
Museau Brawn
Musqué Muscovy duck
Musette, bœuf en Rolled, boned shoulder of beef
Myrtilles Blueberries/Bilberries

Nage Fish stock
Nanette Artichoke hearts, lettuce, mushrooms and truffles
Nantua With crayfish
Napolitaine With horseradish ham and Madeira
Nappé Coating
Natives Oysters
Nature Natural/Plain
Navarin Lamb stew
Navet Turnip/Swede
Nem Spring roll (Asian)
Niçoise Garlic, black olives and olive oil
Ninon With cockscombs and kidney, asparagus and potatoes
Nivernaise With carrots, onions, turnips and lettuce
Noir Black
Noisettes Hazelnuts or small fillet of something (meat)
Noix Walnut
Noix de gigot Leg of mutton
Noix de veau Top side of leg of veal
Noix pâtissière Chump end of loin of veal
Nonat Tiny Mediterranean fish
Noir Black
Noisettes Hazelnuts
Noix Nut
Noix de coco Coconut
Nonnette Flavoured bun
Normande Normandy style
(with cream and cider)
Normande (sauce) Creamy fish sauce
Norvège Norwegian
Nougat Nougat
Nouilles Noodles
Nouveaux New
Nouzillards Name for chestnuts in the Loire area

Tips & Helpful Phrases

Avec With
Sans Without
Bien cuit Well done
Á point Medium
Saignant (e) Rare
De la region Local

USEFUL NOTES:

Oblade Fish similar to bream
Océane Ocean (of the)
Oeuf Eggs
Oeuf à la Monteynard Soft boiled eggs on a bed of rice
Oeufs Bénédictine Poached eggs with hollandaise sauce
Oeufs bourguignonne Eggs poached in red wine
Oeufs brouillés Scrambled eggs
Oeuf coque Soft boiled egg
Oeuf Dur Hard boiled
Oeufs maritchu Scrambled eggs and globe artichokes
Oeuf Mollet Soft boiled
Oeuf au miroir Eggs cooked in butter
Oeuf poché Poached egg
Oeuf sur le plat Fried egg
Oie Goose
Oignons Onions
Oille Casserole of meat and vegetables
Omble chevalier Char fish
Omelette Norvégienne Baked Alaska (ice cream with hot meringue outer casing)
Onctueux Smooth
Onglet Flank of beef
Opéra With chicken livers, asparagus tips and potatoes
Oreillons Ear shaped fried pastry
Orge Barley
Orientale With rice, okra, tomatoes
Origan Oregano
Orléans, consommé Thin chicken soup
Ormeau Abalone (shellfish)
Orphie Garfish, snipe-eel
Ortie Nettles
Os Bone
Oseille Sorrel
Osselet Knuckle bone

Osso bucco Minced meat or fish served in a
hollow bone
Ouliat Onion soup
Oursin Sea Urchin
Ostergruss German Radish
Oyornade Goose in red wine

USEFUL NOTES:

Pagre Similar to sea bream
Paillasson (de pomme de terre) Grated potato
Paille au fromage Cheese straw
Pailleté Crisp fried
Pain Bread
Pain de courgettes Courgette mousse
Pain de mie White loaf
Pain d'épice Ginger bread
Pain perdu French Toast
Paleron Chuck beef
Palet Potato cake
Palette de porc Shoulder of pork
Palmier Pastry biscuit
Paloise With vegetables in hollandaise sauce
Paloise sauce Eggs, butter, onion and mint sauce
Palombe Wood pigeon
Palomet Edible fungus
Palourde Clam
Pamplemousse Grapefruit
Panaché (de) Mixed plate
Panade Bread, milk and cheese soup
Panais Parsnip
Pan bagnat Bread roll with anchovies & salad
Pané Breaded
Panisso A chick pea porridge
Panisses Pea, nut or corn cake with sugar
Pantin Patty filled with pork
Papeton Corn on the cob
Papeton d'aubergines Aubergine baked with egg and cheese
Papillotes Baked in foil/grease proof paper
Parfait Perfect (complete)
Parfait A light ice cream
Parfum Flavour
Paris-brest Filled pastry cake
Parisienne Potatoes, artichokes, tongue and truffles

Parmesan Parmesan Cheese
Parmentier Potato accompaniment
Pastèque Water melon
Patagére Seasonal
Pâté Paté
Pâte Pastry
Pâte à frire Batter
Patate Douce Sweet potato
Pâte brisée Shortcrust pastry
Pâte d'amandes Almond paste
Pâte en croûte Meat pie
Pâte feuilletée Puff pastry
Pâtes Pasta
Pâtes fraîches Fresh pasta
Pâte végétal Vegetable pie
Patte Leg
Pâtisserie French pastry cake
Pâtissière, noix Chump of veal
Patisson Squash or vegetable marrow
Pauchouse a fresh water fish stew
Paupiette Rolled stuffed meat
Pavé Square piece
Paysan (ne) Country style (vegetables)
Peau Skin (peel)
Pebronata de bœuf Braised beef flavoured
with juniper
Pécari Wild pig
Peigne Scallop
Pélamide Fish-like tunny
Pélardon Type of cheese
Pêche Peach
Peler To Peel
Pelure rind/skin
Pépins Seeds
Pépites Nugget
Perche Perch (fish)
Perdreau Partridge (young)
Perdrix Partridge
Père Father
Périgourdine With truffles/pâté

Perles, consommé Thin soup with pearl barley
Perlot Small oyster
Persane With aubergines, onions and tomatoes
Persil Parsley
Persillade Beef salad and parsley
Péruvienne Oxalis, ham and chicken
Petit beurre Butter biscuit
Petit Gris Small snails
Petit Pois Small green peas
Petits fours Small cakes
Petit suisse Cream cheese with sugar
Pétales d'ail Cloves of garlic
Peterram Dish made from sheep's tripe
Petit duc Asparagus, truffles & chicken tartlets
Pétoncles Small scallops
Pets de nonne Sugared fritters
Piballes Small eels
Picarel Small anchovy-like fish
Piece Piece
Pied (de moutons) Lambs Feet
Pied (de porc) Pigs feet
Pied et paquets Trip and trotters casserole
Pigeon Pigeon
Pigeonneau Squab (young pigeon)
Pilet Pintail duck
Pilon Drumstick (chicken)
Pilpil Spicy, hot tomato sauce
Piment Chilli/Capsicum
Pineau Type of wine
Pinée Dried cod
Pignons Pine nuts
Piment doux Capsicum
Piment rouge Chilli pepper
Piment en poudre Chilli powder
Pimprenelle Burnet (brown flowered plant)
Pintade Guinea fowl
Piperade Pepper and onion egg dish
Piqué Pricked

Piquant Hot/spicy
Pissaladière Onion, olive, tomato and anchovies pie
Pissalat Savoury purée
Pistache Pistachio Nut
Pistil de safran Wine sauce
Pistou Pesto
Plantcha Style of cooking with red wine
Plaquemine Persimmon (date/plum)
Pleine Full (complete)
Pleurottes Oyster mushrooms
Plie Plaice
Plouse Fish like cod
Pluie Rained
Poché Poached
Pochouse Fish stew
Poêle Pan Fried
Poêlée Pan fried
Poêlon Casserole
Pointes Tips/points
Pointes d'asperges Asparagus Tips
Poire Pear
Poireau Leek
Pois Peas
Pois carrés Marrowfat peas
Pois Chiche Chick peas
Poisson Fish
Poisson sauteur Regional name for grey mullet
Poitrine Breast/fleshy part
Poivrade Young artichokes eaten with salt
Poivrade (sauce) Vegetable sauce with pepper
Poivre Pepper (pot)
Poivron Pepper (vegetable)
Polenta Thick Maize porridge
Polonaise, sauce With horseradish and butter
Polypore Giant edible fungus
Pommade Thick paste of garlic, herbs & oil

Pomme Apple
Pomme à la Parisienne Tiny nut shapes of potato fried in butter
Pomme anglaise Boiled potatoes
Pomme ananas Pineapple
Pomme château Roast potatoes
Pommé, chou White heart cabbage
Pomme écrasée Crushed potato
Pomme en robe des champs Jacket potato
Pomme frite Chips
Pomme de Terre Potato
Pomme Sarladaises Potato sautéed in garlic and parsley
Pomme Sautée Fried potatoes
Pommes anna Potatoes casseroled in slices
Pommes boulangère Baked around meat joint
Pommes voisin Anna potatoes with cheese
Porc Pork
Porcelet Suckling Pig
Portefeuille Wrapped in pastry
Porto With port wine
Portugaise Tomatoes, mushrooms & garlic
Pot Jug
Pot au Feu Braised meat & veg with broth
Potage Soup
Potage au cari Mulligatawny
Potage bonne femme Leek and potato soup
Potage St Germain Pea soup
Potager Vegetable
Potagère From the casserole
Potée Meat and vegetable stew
Potiquets Small jars
Potiron Pumpkin
Pouding Pudding
Pouding de Noël Christmas pudding
Poudre Powder
Pouillard Young partridge
Poularde Fat Chicken
Poule Hen

Poulet (ette) Chicken
Poulet de Bresse Special chicken from Bresse
Poulpe Octopus
Poupeton Assorted meats rolled
Pourpier Purslane (herb)
Poussin Poussin (young chicken)
Poutargue Dried mullet roll
Poutassou Blue whiting
Praire Clam
Praline Sugared almond
Pratelle Edible mushroom
Pre-cuit Par-boiled
Prête Small sea fish
Primeurs Seasonal fruit/vegetables
Princesse With asparagus, truffles and artichokes
Printanière With mixed vegetables
Prise Taken
Provençale Style of cooking, tomatoes, garlic olives
Prune de damas Damson
Pruneau sec Prune
Prune (aux) Prune
Puree Puree (mashed)

Tips & Helpful Phrases

Je voudrais I would like
Or
Vous avez ? Do you have ?

Quasi de veau Pieces of veal
Quelques Some/a few
Quenelles Dumplings
Quetsche Red plum
Queues Tails
Queue de bœuf Oxtail
Queues de langoustine Tails of Langoustine
or Scampi
Quillet Pastry filled with butter cream
Quintal Type of cabbage

USEFUL NOTES:

Tips & Helpful Phrases

Un couteau Knife
Une fourchette Fork
Une cuillère Spoon
Un verre Glass
Une tasse Cup
Un cendrier Ashtray

USEFUL NOTES:

_____
_____
_____
_____
_____
_____
_____
_____
_____
_____
_____
_____
_____
_____
_____
_____

Rabiole Variety of kohlrabi or turnip
Râble Saddle of rabbit
Rabotte Dumpling
Radis Radishes
Rafraîchi (e) Chilled
Raifort Horseradish
Raie Skate
Rais Skate
Ragoût Ragout/meat stew
Raisins Grapes
Raisin de Corinthe Currants
Raisin de Smyrne Sultanas
Raisin sec Raisins
Raitou Young skate
Ramequin Ramekin (Small cheese bake)
Ramereau Young wood pigeon
Ramier Wood pigeon
Râpé Grated
Rascasse Scorpion Fish (usually in stew)
Ratafia Small macaroon
Ravigotte Vinaigrette of eggs and herbs
Rayon de miel Honeycomb
Recette Recipe
Régence Garnished with meat/fish
dumplings
Régence sauce Chicken based sauce with
ham onions and wine
Réglisse Liquorice
Reine With spring chicken
Reine-claude Greengage plum
Reinettes Type of apple
Réjane With spinach, artichokes, bone
marrow and potatoes
Relevé Spiced up
Rémoulade Mayonnaise with Gherkins,
capers and anchovies
Renaissance With a variety of spring
vegetables
Renne Reindeer/venison

Requin Shark
Resserre Press/clamp for making pate
Rhum Rum
Rhubarbe Rhubarb
Ricotta Type of cheese
Rigadelle Clam
Rillette Serving of potted (meat or fish)
Rillons Crispy meats
Ris Sweetbreads
Ris de veau Sweetbreads with veal
Rivèlle Dumpling
Riz Rice
Riz au blanc Boiled rice
Riz au lait au four Rice pudding
Riz complet Brown rice
Robert (Sauce) Sweet brown onion sauce
Rocamadour Soft goats cheese
Rocambole Spanish garlic
Rochambeau With carrots, lettuce,
cauliflower and potato
Rohan With artichokes, fois gras, truffles
and kidneys
Roitelet Small edible bird
Rognon Kidney
Romaine Type of lettuce
Romanoff With cucumber, mushrooms
and potatoes
Romanoff fraise Strawberries caracao and
cream
Romarin Rosemary
Romsteck Rump steak
Ronde Round
Roquefort Type of cheese
Roquette Rocket
Rosace Rose shaped
Rosbif Roast beef
Rose Pink
Rosette Special sausage made in Lyons
eaten raw
Rôt Roast meat

Rôtengle Freshwater fish
Rôtie Roast
Rouelle Round slice
Rouennais Ducks livers in red wine
Rouennais sauce With beef marrow and duck livers
Rouge Red
Rouge de rivière Wild duck
Rouge-gorge Robin
Rouge-queue Game bird
Rouget Red Mullet
Rouille Mayonnaise made of chillies
Roulade Rolled meat with additives
Rousette Type of fritter
Royan Sardine
Rubané Sliced/layered
Russe (à la) With hard boiled egg, beetroot and sour cream
Rutabaga Swede

USEFUL NOTES:

Tips & Helpful Phrases

Du pain Bread
Du beurre Butter
Du lait Milk
Du sel Salt
De l'eau Water

USEFUL NOTES:

Sabayon Syllabub
Sablé Shortbread
Sacristain Small puff pastry
Safrané Saffron
Sagan Made with risotto
Sagou Sago
Saindoux Lard
Saint Jacques Scallops (shellfish)
Sainte Maure Type of cheese
Saint Pierre John Dory
Saisi Seared
Saisir To sear
Saison Season
Salé (s) Salted
Salicoques Prawns
Salade Salad, lettuce
Salade Cendrillon With celeriac and truffles
Salade Chicago With asparagus & French beans
Salade Composée Mixed salad with meat,
eggs etc
Salade Eve With fruit and cream
Salade Fanchette With chicken, truffles &
mushrooms
Salade Favorite With crayfish and truffles
Salade de fruits Fruit Salad
Salade Isabelle With truffles, celery,
mushrooms and artichokes
Salade de Niçoise Full salad with anchovies
and eggs
Salade Panachée Mixed salad
Salade Paulette With celery, potatoes,
truffles and French beans
Salade Pernollet Crayfish, lettuce, truffles
and asparagus tips
Salade Printanière Mixed grated vegetables
Salade Quercynoise Green salad with duck
meat and raspberry vinegar
Salade Tiède Warm Salad
Salade Tosca Chicken salad with truffles and
parmesan cheese

Salade Tredern Seafood salad
Salambo Choux pastry cake
Sale Salted
Salmis Game bird with wine sauce
Salsifis Salsify (root vegetable)
Salpicon Chopped mixture to be used in sauce, salad or stuffing
Sandré Pike/Perch
Sanglier Boar
Sanguine Blood orange
Sans Without
Sansonnet Starling
Sapin Pine tree
Savarin Type of cake soaked in rum
Sarcelle Teal (Duck)
Sardalaise Potato and truffle accompaniment
Sarments de vigne Vine stems
Sarrasine Buckwheat
Sarriette Savoury
Saucisse Sausage
Saucisson French Sausage
Sauge Sage
Saur Smoked herring
Saurel Type of fish
Sautée à la Chinoise Stir fried
Saupiquet Sharp red wine sauce
Sautoir Sautéed
Saumon Salmon
Saumon Gravlax Cold sliced salmon marinated in dill
Saumon a l'unilatéral Salmon cooked on salt
Sauvages Wild
Savarin Type of cake soaked in rum
Saveurs Flavour
Scare Parrotfish
Schifela Pork with vegetables
Secs Dry
Sèche Dried
Seiche Cuttlefish

Seigle Rye
Sel Salt
Selle Saddle
Selon According to
Selon arrivage If available
Semi-fredo Fruit charlotte
Semoule Semolina
Semoule de mais Polenta
Senteurs Flavours
Serge Artichokes and ham
Serpolet Wild thyme
Servi Served
Sésame Sesame seed
Silure Catfish
Simple Simple/single
Sirop Syrup
Sirop de mais Corn syrup
Sirop d'érable Maple syrup
Smitane sauce Onions and cream
Sobronade Meat soup with vegetables
Socca Chickpea
Soins (par nos soins) With care
Soissons White haricot beans
Soja Soya
Sole Dover sole
Son de blé Bran
Sorbet Sorbet
Sorgho Sorghum
Sot l'y laisse Parsons nose
Sou fassum Stuffed cabbage
Soubise White sauce
Soufflé Soufflé
Soupe Soup
Soupions Baby cuttlefish
Souris (d'agneau) Lamb shank
Sous Bois Under growth
Spetzi Dumpling
Squille Type of fish
Sterlet Baby sturgeon
Stoemp Mashed potato and vegetable

Streusel Cake
Sucrin Melon
Sucre Sugar
Suédoise Layered fruit jelly
Suif Suet
Suprême Breast
Surimi Crab
Surmulet Red mullet

Tips & Helpful Phrases

je suis allérgique á
I am allergic to
Aux Noix Nuts
Aux fruits de mer Shellfish
Au blé Wheat
Aux œufs Eggs
Aux avocats Avocado

Je suis végétarien (ienne)
I am vegetarian

Je suis diabétique
I am diabetic

Taboulé Salad with bulgar wheat, chilli, lemon and garlic
Tacaud Type of cod
Taillée Cut
Tajine African Stew
Taliburs Pastry bake
Talleyrand Truffles, macaroni and foie gras accompaniment
Tanche Tench
Tanagra With celery, tomatoes, bananas and sour cream
Tapenade Olives, capers, anchovies in a paste
Tarama Taramasalata
Tartine Sliced bread and butter
Tarte Pie/Tart
Tarte Tatin Upside down apple pie
Tartelette Small tart
Tasse Cup
Tatin Upside down pie
Taupe Type of fish
Tendon Knuckle
Tendre Tender
Terrine Bowl
Terrine Loaf of fish/meat (similar to pâté)
Testard Chub
Têtard Young goat
Tête (de veau) Brains (of calf)
Tétras Grouse
Thés Tea
Tinamou Game bird
Thoionnade Toast spread with garlic/tomato
Thon Tuna
Thym Thyme
Tian Gratin (usually of) fish/vegetables in a shallow dish
Tiède Warm
Tilleul Lime
Timbale Dish for pies

Tivoli With asparagus, mushrooms and kidneys of fowl
Tocan Small salmon
Tomate Tomatoes
Tombe Gurnard
Topinambour Artichoke (Jerusalem)
Torchon Food compressed in a cloth
Torpille Type of fish
Torsade Plaited
Tourin Onion soup
Torta Aniseed cake
Tourteau fromagé Light cheese/sponge cake
Touraine Tomato, onion and egg soup with crouton
Touraine Blanchi Traditional Garlic Soup/boiled fowl
Touraine, géline de Type of fowl
Tourangelle Hazelnut oil
Tournedos Steak
Tournesol Sunflower
Tourte Pie
Tourte à la lorraine Veal and pork quiche
Tourteau Type of crab
Tourtière Meat pie
Toscane Macaroni and truffle accompaniment
Toulia Onion soup
Toulousaine Chicken and mushroom accompaniment
Tout All/Complete
Tourte Pie/Tart with puff pastry
Traité Treated (Cooked)
Tranche Slice
Tranche napolitaine Mixed flavoured ice cream
Travers de porc Spare ribs
Tremper To dip
Trévise Radicchio (salad leaves)
Trigle Gurnet

Tripa Spinach sausage
Tripes Tripe
Tripette Fried sheep's intestines
Tripoux Sheep's trotters
Tripous Tripe
Trognon Vegetable heart (or fruit)
Tronçon Thick slice or piece
Trou normand Palate freshener (drink
between courses)
Troupeaux Herds (of animals)
Trouvillaise Seafood and mushroom
accompaniment
Truffade Accompaniment of potatoes,
bacon, cheese and garlic
Truffé With truffle
Truffes Truffles
Truite Trout
Trumeau Leg or skirt of beef
Tuile Thin Wafer
Tuiles Almond biscuits
Tyrolienne With tomatoes and onions
Tzarine With cream and cucumbers

USEFUL NOTES:

_____

_____

_____

_____

_____

_____

_____

_____

_____

_____

_____

Tips & Helpful Phrases

Je ne comprend pas
I do not understand

Parlez vous Anglaise?
Do you speak English

Ou et la toilette s'il vous plait?
Where is the toilet please?

W.C. S'il vous plait?
(W.C. is pronounced
VAY SAY)

USEFUL NOTES:

Unilatéral See Saumon a l'unilatéral
Vache Cow
Vacherin Meringue filled with fruit and cream
Vacherin glacé Ice cream cake
Valenciennes With peppers and rice
Valois With potatoes and artichokes
Valse Waltz (of oysters)
Vanille Vanilla
Vapeur Steamed
Variation Alternatives
Veau Veal (calf)
Velouté Soft/smooth – creamed as in soup
Venaison Venison
Venaison, basse Hare
Vendangeurs Grape pickers
Verre Glass
Verdette Edible fungus
Verdure Greenery
Verrine Glass Bowl
Verjus Juice of unripe grapes
Vernon Vegetable purée
Véron sauce Rich veal sauce with herbs
Vert Green
Verte Mayonnaise with spinach
Verveine Lemon herb
Verveine Aromatic marinade
Vessie Sausage
Viande Meat
Viande Séchée Dried Cured Meat
Vichy Carrots
Vichyssoise Cream of leek soup
Victoria sauce Lobster sauce
Viennoise With noodles
Vierge (sauce) Virgin (Sauce)
Vieux Old
Vigneronne Grapes with wine sauce
Villeroi sauce Ham and truffles sauce
Vin Wine

Vinaigre Vinegar
Vinaigrette Oil and vinegar dressing
Violet Shell fish (clam)
Vive Weever fish
Viveurs, consommé Duck flavoured soup
Viviane potage Chicken and vegetable soup
Vivaneau Red snapper
Vivier Fish tank
Voilé Spun sugar
Volaille Poultry
Volaille, gelée de Cold jellied soup

Acknowledgement

Thanks to Monica Taylor, Holly Sutcliffe,
Maureen McDonnell, Amelia Jackson, Sandra Taylor
and Sandrine Dechosal, all of whom have helped
me with the publication of this book.

Walewska Crayfish tails
Waterzooï Chicken stew
Xérès Sherry
Yaourt Yoghurt
Zabaglione Zabaglione (type of mousse)
Zampino Stuffed trotter
Zee forgeron John dory fish
Zeste Zest (lemon peel)
Zelma Kuntz Fruit puree and praline
Zewelwai Onion flan

W
X
Y
Z

USEFUL NOTES:

_____

_____

_____

_____

_____

_____

_____

_____

_____

_____

_____

_____

_____

_____

_____

_____

_____

_____

_____

NOTES

NOTES

NOTES